Everything You Need to Know About

DRUG ADDICTION

The best way to avoid a potential drug addiction is to avoid using drugs at all.

Everything You Need to Know About

DRUG ADDICTION

Jeanne M. Nagle

THE ROSEN PUBLISHING GROUP, INC.
NEW YORK

Published in 1999 by The Rosen Publishing Group, Inc.
29 East 21st Street, New York, NY 10010

Copyright © 1999 by The Rosen Publishing Group, Inc.

First Edition

Library of Congress Cataloging-in-Publication Data

Nagle, Jeanne M.
        Everything you need to know about drug addiction / Jeanne M. Nagle
                p.   cm. — (The need to know library)
        Includes bibliographical references and and index.
        Summary: Discusses the nature of addictions, some of the substances—
including illegal and prescription drugs, alcohol, caffeine, and steroids—to which
people become addicted, and how to get help.
        ISBN 0-8239-2772-5
        1. Drug abuse—Juvenile literature. 2. Narcotic habit—Juvenile
literature. [1. Drug abuse.] I. Title. II. Title: about drug addiction.
III. Series.
HV5809.5.N34 1998
362.29--dc21   98-45102
                                                                                CIP
                                                                                 AC

Manufactured in the United States of America

Contents

Introduction

Long after everyone had gone to bed, Jen sat alone in the dark kitchen with a glass of vodka. She had poured only a little so that her parents wouldn't notice that any was missing. Besides, she didn't need much, just enough to help her sleep.

Things had been pretty rough lately. Six months earlier, her boyfriend, Chris, had broken up with her. She knew it was really all over a week later, when she had seen him at a party hanging all over Tracy Miller, who was getting wasted on beer and Jell-O shots.

Fine, Jen had thought, if that's the kind of girl guys want, that's what I'll be. She had grabbed one of the small plastic cups from the table and popped the jiggling shot into her mouth. It tasted like regular gelatin, only with a kick of vodka. She quickly finished four more, and then she began to feel weird. The shots had gone down so easily that at first she didn't realize she was getting drunk.

Soon Jen didn't care where Chris was or who he was with. She was busy flirting with other guys at the party. People who had never paid attention to her before were acting like her friends now. The alcohol made her feel relaxed and confident.

From then on, Jen always had a few drinks whenever she started to feel bad about not being with Chris. Or if school was starting to get on her nerves. Or if her parents were on her case about breaking curfew. There was always a bottle or two at parties, or she and her new friends would sneak some wine coolers or beers from home and drink them in the park by the school. Forgetting about her problems for a while was worth the sick stomach and headache she sometimes had the next day.

Tonight Jen was having trouble sleeping. She decided that a couple of drinks would help her relax and get some sleep. No big deal. It wasn't like she was passed out in the street or anything.

Jen finished her glass of vodka and, since she wasn't really sleepy, decided to have just a little bit more. What harm could it do?

Some people use drugs, such as alcohol, with the misplaced hope that it will make them feel better or help them get through a hard time.

Chapter 1

What Is Addiction?

Nobody makes a conscious decision to become a drug addict. A person who uses alcohol or drugs can become addicted without even realizing it.

According to the American Heritage Dictionary, an addict is someone who has given over. In other words, people who are addicted give up power over who they are and how they act to someone or something else. It's like being a prisoner and being told what to do and when to do it. Becoming addicted also means being dependent, which is the direct opposite of the independence we all want as young adults.

Ever heard the expression *a bottomless pit?* That's what an addiction is. Addicts can never get enough of a drug. They are always hungry for more. Nothing, not even an endless supply of the thing they crave, can fill them up.

A person who is addicted cannot control her drug use.

There are several kinds of addiction. A person can be addicted to gambling, continuing to bet after losing hundreds, even thousands, of dollars. He can be addicted to food, sex, or exercise. One of the most common addictions in the United States is to drugs and alcohol.

Addiction as a Disease

It is easy to think that addiction could be overcome or avoided by using willpower. After all, there are people who drink alcohol, take prescribed medicines, or even use illegal drugs, who do not become addicted. Those who do get hooked must be weak, right?

Researchers and doctors don't think that's necessarily the case. They say that addiction is a disease.

If a germ or some other foreign invader gets inside you and changes the way your mind or body acts, you may have a disease. Diseases can make you feel sick, take all your energy, and make you sad or depressed. They can even kill you.

Addiction works the same way. Think of the drug or alcohol as the germ that causes a disease by changing the way a person's mind and body work. Once someone is addicted, he needs the drug to feel normal. When he doesn't take the drug, he doesn't feel right. Not getting another fix can make a person completely depressed. Drug addiction can also kill a person, as in an overdose, when someone takes too much of a drug.

Some people may argue that nobody wants to get the disease of addiction, but those who use drugs bring addiction on themselves. It is important to remember that addiction is not a choice. Yes, experimenting with drugs, which is often how addiction starts, is a choice. But once a drug takes hold, it is difficult for a person to keep addiction from occurring.

The disease of addiction requires patience and hard work to control. But it can be overcome.

Drug Abuse vs. Drug Addiction

Experts agree that there is a difference between drug abuse and drug addiction. Drug abuse is using a substance in a way other than it is meant to be used. For instance, cleaning fluid is meant to clean things. Sniffing it to get high is abuse. Some drugs, such as heroin, have no common use. Simply using them at all is abuse.

Another way to abuse a drug is to take more than you should. Examples include taking five pills when the label on the bottle says to take only one, or taking a pill every hour when you're supposed to wait six hours before the next dose. Even a drug as common as aspirin can be abused.

In drug addiction, on the other hand, people abuse drugs over and over, to the point at which the drug use actually changes the way their brains work. The addicted brain "learns" that drugs can not only temporarily make you feel good, but that they are necessary to life, like breathing. Eventually people who are addicted take drugs not just to get high, but to feel normal.

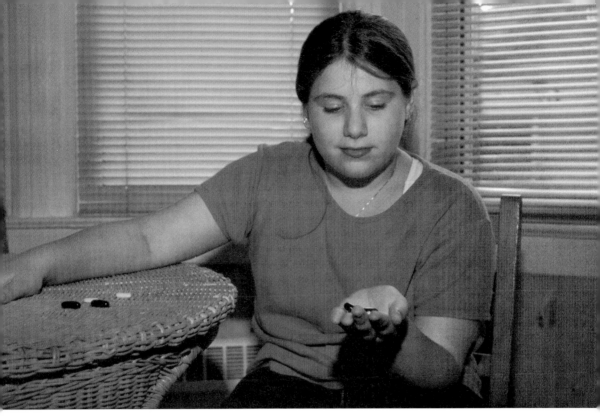

Your mind or your body may become so used to a drug that it needs the drug to feel normal.

To a drug abuser, not taking the drug may mean disappointment. For those who are addicted, not taking a drug can result in painful withdrawal symptoms.

Who Is at Risk?

Doctors and scientists have conducted many surveys and tests to determine whether some people are more likely to become addicted to drugs and alcohol than others. They found several factors that put kids at risk of addiction:

- Having parents who abuse drugs or alcohol, now or in the past
- Having parents who are sick, absent, unemployed, or abusive

13

- Being too aggressive, in class or at home
- Feeling hurt or neglected
- Performing poorly in school
- Not being able to make friends easily
- Hanging out with friends who do drugs

Some studies show that genetics may also play a part in addiction. People are born with certain levels of chemicals in their brains, creating a balance that helps determine their personality. When new chemicals like drugs are added, that balance is upset. How the normal chemicals react with a drug's chemicals can determine how quickly and to what extent a person becomes addicted to different substances.

While some people may have more of a tendency to become addicted, the truth is that anyone can become addicted to drugs or alcohol. Addiction is a disease like any other. Addiction is a result of chemical changes in the brains of drug users caused by the drugs they are using.

Chapter 2

How Addiction Works

Human beings learn early about rewards for certain kinds of behavior. Parents may say things like, "Eat all your dinner and you can have dessert," or, "Do your chores and you can take the car on Saturday." At work, people hear, "You've done such a good job, we're giving you a raise."

The brain operates on a reward system too. Our brains have natural chemicals called neurotransmitters. These send messages that determine how we feel and react. When we do something rewarding, such as getting an A on a test, our brain releases chemicals that make us feel good. This is how our natural chemical reward system works.

The brain has a specialized pathway of nerve cells to relay messages about pleasure called the pleasure circuit. Many drugs activate the brain's pleasure circuit.

The brain naturally releases certain chemicals when something good happens. These chemicals make you feel happy.

Unfortunately, the more a person uses drugs to get that feeling of pleasure, the more the brain depends on drugs.

The Cycle of Addiction

Eventually, if a person takes a drug often enough, the brain changes so that it can handle all the extra chemicals that are being put into it. In order to adjust, the brain tells the neurotransmitters to slow down the release of certain chemicals in the pleasure circuit. As a result, normal levels of chemicals are too low. When that happens, a person becomes depressed. The person then takes more of the drug in order to feel better.

The drug addict does feel better, but only for a short time. The extra chemicals from the drug again tell the brain to stop producing its own chemicals, which further reduces normal levels. When the high wears off, the addict feels even worse than before. This is called withdrawal. That person craves another fix to help him feel better, and the cycle starts all over again.

Our bodies have a system of checks and balances that keep us from being too happy, too sad, too stressed out—too anything. In a way, it's as if we have an electrical circuit board in our brain that determines how much of various neurotransmitters we need in certain situations. When it gets the signal, the brain then produces the correct amount. Drugs and alcohol act like a power surge, overloading the brain with chemicals. Just as an electrical power surge can blow up a computer or turn off all the lights, drugs cause problems with the chemicals in our brains. This causes addiction, in which the brain can no longer function without a drug.

The Pattern of Addiction

Most people who become addicted to drugs follow a similar pattern of addiction.

> 1. First, you experiment with drugs. People first take drugs for many reasons. You may try drugs because of pressures at home, coaxing from friends, or curiosity about how a drug will make you feel.

2. Your tolerance increases. The more of a chemical you use, the more of that chemical you will
   need to get the same effect.

3. You may have blackouts. There may be times
   when you do not remember what you did when
   you were drinking or using drugs.

4. You avoid talking about about drugs or alcohol. As your addiction develops, you try to take
   attention away from anything that will point it
   out.

5. You become preoccupied with drug use. You
   spend time thinking about drugs, plan your use
   carefully, and choose your friends based on
   drugs.

6. You blame others and make excuses for your
   drug use. You may even cause fights as an
   excuse to drink. This stage is called denial.

7. You lose control of your drug use. You cannot
   control how much you use or stop yourself
   from taking more. You may feel weak or think
   that you do not have willpower.

8. Your drug use affects your family, friends, and
   education. It may destroy your relationships.
   You may skip school to use your drug.

9. You may have medical, legal, or psychiatric problems.

10. You lose hope. As your addiction gets worse, you may feel as though there is nothing you can do to stop it. You may feel as if your life has lost its meaning or is not worth living.

Why People Take Drugs

Lamar remembers what it was like to feel left out. It was not too long ago that, as the new kid at school, he felt that he didn't belong anywhere. After all, he wasn't a jock, so he couldn't hang with those guys. His grades were decent, but he wasn't a brain either. He didn't think it was smart to get involved with the kids he pegged as gang members, or at least wannabes.

Then, while taking a shortcut home from school one day, he ran into a kid named Ray and a group of Ray's friends. They were out behind the field house on the football field, having a smoke. Because of Ray's reputation, Lamar knew those weren't regular cigarettes they were passing around.

Lamar tried to be cool and ignore them, but Ray called out to him. "Hey," he said, "how about a toke?" His friends laughed, because they knew Ray was testing Lamar. They didn't think he'd come over and join them.

But Lamar knew it was a dare, and he didn't want them to laugh at him. "Sure," he said, walking right up to Ray. He'd never tried marijuana before, but he'd been around other kids who had. He'd seen how you held a joint and knew that you were supposed to keep the smoke in as long as you could to get the best buzz. Besides, he'd smoked cigarettes before, and how different could it be?

Lamar took a long drag on the joint. He tried to hold the smoke in, but there was too much, and it burned his throat. He let it out right away, and then started hacking.

Ray and his guys were laughing like crazy, and Lamar figured he'd made a fool of himself. Instead, Ray slapped him on the back a couple of times and offered him the joint again. Lamar laughed at himself, too, and quickly took a smaller hit off the joint.

From then on Ray and his buddies would nod at Lamar in the hall and let him sit with them at lunch and free periods. One week they went to a ball game together. Lamar had finally found a place to belong. The only price was smoking a little weed now and then.

Lamar remembers what it was like to feel lonely and not to have friends. He's glad those days are over.

There are several reasons why someone might experiment with drugs or alcohol. Some teens, like Lamar, try them because of peer pressure. Their friends encourage them to try drugs in order to fit in. Other teens experiment because they think drugs will help them deal with their problems or make their problems go away. Some teens experiment with drugs or alcohol simply because they're curious, or just plain bored.

After experimenting, a person might start to use drugs more regularly. Using drugs becomes a routine

Resisting peer pressure to try drugs is difficult. You must care
more about yourself than what other people think.

part of his life, a habit. It's something he does over and over without thinking.

With repeated (also known as chronic) drug use, a person can become dependent on the drug. Drugs become not just an occasional part of life, but as necessary as food or water. Addicts plan their lives around drugs: working or stealing to get money to buy more, setting their schedules so that they can get a fix, ignoring friends and family. A person who is dependent on drugs cannot stop taking them. He is addicted. Taking drugs matters more than anything else the person has ever done or believed. Someone who is addicted will lie, cheat, steal—perhaps even kill—to get another hit.

Psychological and Physical Addiction

There are two kinds of addiction: psychological and physical.

Psychological Addiction

When a person believes that he needs drugs to survive, he is psychologically addicted, or dependent.

The location and situations in which a person does drugs play a large role in psychological addiction. A user may associate certain actions or rituals with taking drugs. If a person smokes marijuana every time she goes to a party, eventually she will not be able to go to a party without lighting up a joint, or at least feeling very strongly that she needs to smoke one.

A person may crave alcohol when he hangs out with the people he usually drinks with.

Physical Addiction

Physical addiction happens when a person's mind and body change so much that they need the drug in order to function normally. It is possible to be psychologically addicted to drugs without being physically dependent.

When a physically addicted person takes a drug for a while, she begins to build up a tolerance for it. Her body and brain come to accept certain levels of the substance as normal—they tolerate the drug. The amount of the drug it once took to get high no longer works. Larger and more frequent doses are needed for the user to feel the effects.

A person who is physically addicted to a drug suffers from withdrawal when she doesn't get the drug. During withdrawal she may sweat, hallucinate (see things that aren't there), vomit, or shake uncontrollably.

Cravings are a sign of both psychological and physical dependence. A craving is like being hungry, only a user is hungry for a certain thing—in this case, the drug—and the feeling is much more intense. People who crave a drug are desperate to take it.

Chapter 3

Addictive Drugs and Their Effects

Many types of drugs, both legal and illegal, are abused by people. Many of these drugs are physically addictive, and all have the potential to be psychologically addictive. Prescription drugs have medicinal value and are legally prescribed by doctors to cure illness and treat diseases. "Street drugs" such as crack cocaine, marijuana, and LSD have no medical use and can only be sold illegally. Other drugs, such as nicotine and alchohol, while having no medicinal value, are sold legally because they are endorsed by society.

Many drugs can be classified—put into groups—according to the effects that they produce in the brain.

Stimulants

Stimulants act on the central nervous system. Common stimulants include cocaine, crack (a form of cocaine

Exhaustion is a common side effect of depressants.

that is smoked), and prescription amphetamines such as Dexedrine and Benzedrine, which are most commonly prescribed for obese people to aid in weight loss. Increased energy and concentration are common side effects. The user feels less tired and bored. An overall positive outlook can also be a result.

The downside is that stimulants can make a person irritable, overly aggressive, and nervous. Because they keep the user awake, they often lead to insomnia—the inability to fall or stay asleep. Stimulants may also cause nausea, headaches, sweating, and mild shaking.

People addicted to stimulants often take these

drugs in binges. They take large amounts for periods of time, and then stop for a while. Binges are common because the effects of the drugs don't last very long. Frequent doses are needed to keep a high going.

Both the nicotine in tobacco and the caffeine in certain drinks and foods are addictive stimulants. Both drugs (and they really are drugs) make users more alert.

Most people don't think addiction to these drugs is very serious, but it can have negative consequences. Too much caffeine—from coffee, tea, soft drinks, or chocolate—can make a person feel nervous or restless. Mild shaking, throbbing headaches, and exhaustion are possible side effects.

In 1988, the Surgeon General released a report saying that, "cigarettes and other forms of tobacco are just as addicting as heroin and cocaine." The addictive chemical in tobacco is nicotine. As a main ingredient in cigarettes, cigars, and chewing tobacco, it gets people hooked on smoking or chewing tobacco, which can cause heart disease and cancer after years of use. Withdrawal symptoms of nicotine addiction usually include strong cravings, difficulty concentrating, and feelings of sensitivity, anger, and tiredness.

Depressants

Depressants slow down the central nervous system. Prescription depressants include barbiturates, such as Seconal and phenobarbital; and benzodiazepines, such as Valium and Xanax. Doctors prescribe certain depressants, such as Valium or Xanax, to help people relax or sleep. Taken in larger doses, depressants can make a person act drunk. Common side effects include slurred speech, blurred vision, difficulty concentrating, drowsiness, and memory loss. Over time, people addicted to depressants may also suffer from painful muscle aches and permanent problems with coordination.

It's pretty easy to get hooked on depressants. Withdrawal symptoms range from mild—insomnia and restlessness—to severe, which include mental confusion and seizures. The worst cases of withdrawal can result in coma or death.

Alcohol is one of the most widely used legal, addictive drugs. Even though it can make a person seem relaxed and happy, alcohol is actually a depressant. In fact, it can depress the activity of the central nervous system so much that, when a person is really drunk, he or she passes out.

Brain damage, memory loss, sleep disorders, and the possibility of seizures are potential problems associated with alcohol addiction. The liver and heart are also affected, as are the stomach and the intestines.

Hallucinogens

Hallucinogens, also called psychedelics, affect the senses. Hallucinogens include drugs such as LSD, mescaline, PCP (angel dust), and "magic" mushrooms. They change the way a person sees, hears, and smells things. Colors look brighter, and objects become very vivid and may

A person who is psychologically addicted to marijuana may feel unable to function without it.

take on different shapes. Users hear voices or see things that are not really there.

Getting high on hallucinogens is called tripping. Some users wrongly believe that a good trip can create deep thoughts and pleasant experiences. A bad trip can result in severe paranoia, with the user thinking she is in grave danger and that everybody is out to get her.

Two of the greatest dangers of hallucinogens are overdose and accidents. An overdose is when someone takes so much of a drug that the body can't handle it. Users of hallucinogens often become so disoriented that they have difficulty judging time and distance. It is not uncommon for users to accidentally hurt themselves in such impaired conditions.

Driving while under the influence of alcohol or drugs often
leads to fatal accidents.

Narcotics

Narcotics, or opiates, are usually derived from the opium poppy. Narcotics include morphine, codeine, opium, and heroin (smack). Some kinds of narcotics, including morphine and codeine, are prescribed by doctors for use as painkillers. These drugs, however, are highly addictive, and doctors monitor their use very closely.

People who abuse narcotics often want to numb themselves to the rest of the world. They may act as if they are in a dream. Negative side effects include a severe lack of motivation, low sex drive, lack of caring for family or friends, and accidents caused by unclear thinking. For instance, a person could cut himself so deeply that he'd need stitches but fail to realize how bad the injury was because narcotics had diminished the pain and the urge to get help.

Cannabinoids

Cannabinoids is another name for marijuana (pot) and hashish (hash). Users of these drugs often experience trouble with memory, concentration, and coordination. They also tend to be apathetic, meaning they just don't seem to care. High doses can create paranoia, hallucinations, and panic. Experts believe that although there is little evidence of physical addiction, marijuana can cause a strong psychological addiction.

Inhalants

Sniffing fumes has been a common way of getting "high" for a long time. The practice dates back at least to the 1800s, when people inhaled the anesthetic ether. Sniffing was pretty popular in the 1960s, too, when model airplane glue and nail polish remover were the inhalant, or fume source, of choice.

Many inhalants used today are products made from natural gas and petroleum. These include cleaning or lighter fluid, gasoline, rubber cement, correction fluid, and even felt-tipped pens. Items in aerosol cans are often used too.

Inhaled vapors, which act as a sedative, are absorbed quickly by the body and are eliminated slowly. The high from these drugs makes a person feel dizzy and can cause nausea, drooling, sneezing, coughing, and problems with reflexes. Liver, kidney, and brain damage are not uncommon. Because the vapors can also slow down breathing and disturb the heart rate, a person can suffocate or die from heart failure when inhaling.

Steroids

Steroids are a synthetic version of the male hormone testosterone. The natural hormone testosterone is responsible for men's features like thick body hair, deep voices, and muscle growth. Some people take steroids to enhance muscle growth. Athletes in particular take steroids in the hope of becoming stronger and faster.

While steroids seem to have positive results, they have plenty of drawbacks. Because the drugs also keep bones from developing normally, their use can stop the body from growing. Heart, liver, and kidney diseases can occur. Tendons, which connect muscles to bones, become brittle and fragile, like old rubber bands, and can break easily. Steroids also tend to make people very aggressive and potentially violent.

Men who abuse steroids can lose signs of their maleness. Some men's testicles shrink; others grow breasts that look like a woman's. Women, on the other hand, start to look more masculine when they abuse steroids. Their breasts may shrink and their voices get deeper. The testosterone causes problems with a woman's reproductive system, and can prevent her from bearing children.

All drugs have the potential to be psychologically addictive, and many are physically addictive as well. Whether a drug is legal or illegal has little to do with its addictive qualities. A drug prescribed by a doctor can be just as addictive as one obtained illegally on the street. Drugs that are accepted by society, such as nicotine and alcohol, are no less addictive than illegal drugs.

Chapter 4

The Price of Addiction

Research into addiction has shown that people hooked on drugs or alcohol experience similar problems. Generally, their lives get worse instead of better. Negative side effects, such as withdrawal symptoms, damage to the brain and body, and loss of control over one's life are all risks associated with addiction. But they are not the only dangers.

What's more, it's not only the user who is affected by drug addiction. Addiction is a societal problem. Family, friends, strangers, and whole communities can be touched by the actions and problems of one addicted person.

Health Hazards

Besides negative side effects and withdrawal symptoms, drug addiction poses other health risks to the addict. Addiction to drugs that are injected with needles, such as heroin and methamphetamine, are of particular concern. In their hurry to get a fix, sometimes people use needles that have already been used or are dirty in some other way. Dirty needles can make a person sick because they carry germs, which the user puts into his bloodstream. A user can contract tetanus, hepatitis (liver disease), or HIV from dirty needles.

Another problem is that illegal substances are not regulated, as prescription medicines are. Because the pills and injections you get from a doctor or pharmacist are carefully created, there is very little risk that, when taken properly, they will hurt anyone.

That is not true with street drugs. You never know what you're getting when you buy drugs on the street. The people who make and sell them are not careful about what goes into them. They sometimes cut, or add, extra stuff into the drugs to increase the amount of drug they have to sell. Cocaine and heroin may be cut with other powdery ingredients, such as sugar or starch. These things are not dangerous to ingest, but other substances used for cutting may be. Dealers are not above using ingredients such as drain cleaner to mix with cocaine.

Economic Losses

It takes money to buy drugs, legal or illegal. Some may seem inexpensive—at first. But an addict needs drugs often. The money spent adds up pretty quickly, since the user is constantly buying to feed his or her habit.

Drug addicts often have a hard time holding on to jobs. They become distracted by their cravings or by drug use. They miss days, then lose jobs. They are left without money for the drugs they crave, or for such necessities as food and a place to live.

Society, too, feels the money crunch brought on by addiction. Homeowners and shopkeepers lose money when people who are addicted rob them. Employers pay sick time and lose productivity when people who are addicted don't show up for work or cause accidents on the job because they're under the influence of drugs. Taxpayers pay for prisons, where many drug addicts and dealers end up.

The hidden costs of addiction are paid not just by the addict, but by family and friends as well.

People Problems

People addicted to drugs generally have interpersonal problems, or trouble dealing with others. They argue with their parents or friends, often about drug use itself. Sometimes an addict may shut himself off and become a loner or a runaway, or look to a group of friends who don't nag him about using drugs (usually other drug users) rather than fight all the time.

A drug addict is also often unable to get things done. You can't count on someone who is addicted. People who suffer from addiction spend most of their time thinking about or actually getting the next fix. As a result, they often let other matters slip. Grades drop,

Dealers may cut heroin or cocaine with substances that are poinsonous to the human body, such as household cleaners.

they miss work, and friends drift away because the addicted person can't follow through on his or her promises.

Many drug addicts have low self-esteem. Fighting with or rejecting friends and family, and being seen as a failure because of bad grades or losing a job, can easily make a person believe that he or she isn't worth much. Often these people then use drugs to help lift their spirits. But what they're actually doing is making matters worse.

Addiction and Crime

Nikko couldn't believe this was happening. It was supposed to be a night out with the guys, going to hear his favorite band. He never expected to be spending it in jail.

Everything had been fine earlier. Nikko had gotten off work and picked up Miguel and Todd, and the three of them took off for the auditorium. He was tired, but really psyched about hearing some tunes. Before the concert, they bought some cocaine in the parking lot. Nikko was glad he was able to score some coke, because he had run out and really had a taste for it now, especially since he was so tired. He, Miguel, and Todd had a little pick-me-up party in the car, snorting a few lines before the concert. Nikko stashed the extra vial in his jacket pocket for later.

On their way into the auditorium, some guy bumped into Miguel. Miguel was high and unsteady on his feet. He fell to the floor. Nikko and Todd got really angry; all they saw was Miguel fall to the floor. Figuring the other guy hit Miguel, Nikko shoved him. The guy punched him back.

Nikko didn't remember much of the fight after that, except that somebody went through a glass door at the auditorium. After that happened, police were suddenly all over the place. They broke up the fight and hauled everyone down to the station.

It was bad enough being booked on disorderly conduct. Then the cops found the extra vial of cocaine in Nikko's jacket pocket. He was put in a holding cell, where he waited to see if his parents would come bail him out.

Plain and simple, crime and drug addiction go together. Using, dealing, or just possessing illegal drugs can land you in jail.

Things that were once important, such as school, friends, and family, may seem less important as a person becomes addicted to drugs.

Along with those offenses, property crime—which includes robbery, theft, and breaking and entering—accounts for the largest part of crime associated with addiction. This is mostly because users frequently steal to get money for drugs. Vandalism, in which property is destroyed or marked up, is also a concern.

Violent crime is also connected to drug addiction. It includes the crimes of battery, rape, and murder. Violent crime often happens because drugs cloud the user's judgment and make him or her very aggressive. That results in fights, and possibly murder. While robbing a store, someone who is addicted might kill or be killed by the shop owner or police.

Violent crime is also a part of the lifestyle associated with drugs. Someone may get hurt or killed because he owes money to a dealer or is involved in a drug deal that goes bad.

Domestic violence is yet another crime often connected to drug addiction, especially when the drug is alcohol. Studies show that alcohol abuse is frequently a contributing factor in family violence, particularly against a spouse.

Alcohol also makes some people very aggressive, which allows them to become verbally abusive. Such obnoxious behavior can start fights and result in injuries.

On top of all that, addiction increases the chance of the user's becoming a victim of crime. Drugs numb people's minds and affect their decision-making skills.

Drug use can cause people to do things they wouldn't normally do. Some of those things, such as fighting, can even result in a person's arrest.

When you're drunk or stoned, it's easier for criminals to take advantage of you, because you don't think, communicate, or react normally.

Addiction has many prices. It can cost you your friends, your family, your money, your health, and even your life. The small amount of pleasure that drugs provide cannot make up for the pains of addiction.

Chapter 5

Self-Assessment

Knowing the facts about drugs is important, but analyzing your attitudes and behaviors toward alcohol and drug use helps when making careful decisions for yourself.

The following questions, provided by the Alcohol and Drug Education Center of the University of Utah, can help you decide whether you have a problem with drugs or alcohol. Answer as honestly as possible. All questions include the use of legal and illegal drugs.

- Are you unable to stop drinking or dosing after a certain number of drinks/doses?
- Do you need a drink/drug to get motivated?
- Do you often forget what happened while you were partying?
- Do you drink/use drugs alone?

- Have others annoyed you by questioning your drinking or drug use?
- Have you been involved in fights while you were drunk or high?
- Have you done or said anything while drinking or using drugs that you regretted?
- Have you destroyed or damaged property while drinking or using drugs?
- Have you been physically hurt while under the influence of drugs or alcohol?
- Have you been in trouble with school officials or the police?
- Have you dropped or chosen friends based on their drinking/drug habits?
- Do you think you are a normal drinker/drug-taker despite friends' comments that you drink or use drugs too much?
- Have you ever missed classes or work because you were too hungover to get up on time?
- Have you ever done poorly on an exam or an assignment because of drinking or drug use?
- Do you often think about drinking or getting high?
- Do your social activities have to involve drinking or the use of drugs in order for you to enjoy yourself?
- Do you think that drinking or drug use is affecting your ability to maintain healthy, intimate relationships with a boyfriend/girlfriend?

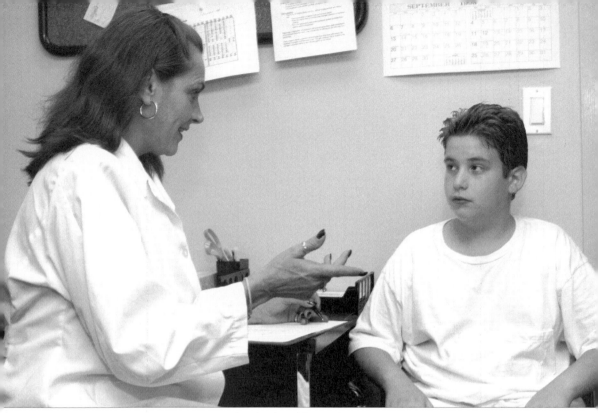

Talking to someone who is familiar with drug and alcohol abuse, such as a guidance counselor, can help you determine whether or not you have a problem with drugs or alcohol.

- Do you think that drinking or drug use is affecting your physical health on an ongoing basis?
- Do you believe you need to drink or use a drug (other than those prescribed) to function at work, school, home, or in social situations?

If you answered yes to one or more of these questions, or you are concerned about your use, you may be using alcohol or drugs in a way that is harmful. But don't panic. Talk with someone about your worries and seek help if you think it's necessary.

Whatever you do, don't give up hope. Addiction is a serious problem, but it's not unbeatable.

Chapter 6

Treatment

The good news about addiction is that there are ways to get help. Treatment can be difficult, both to start and to keep on track, but recovery is certainly possible.

Addicts who recognize their addiction are the easiest to help. They see that they are hurting themselves and those around them and want to do something about it.

But more commonly, addicted people cannot admit (or maybe don't even realize) that they have a problem. They don't want to look weak or out of control. To cover themselves, they make up excuses for their behavior. They lie to others and to themselves that everything is fine and that they have themselves under control. This is called denial. Denial is powerful, almost as powerful as the addiction. One way to help an addicted person recognize his or her addiction is to confront him or her with the facts.

Intervention

You can help an addicted person admit that he or she has a problem through an intervention. This is when a small group of individuals who care for and support a person confront that person with his or her addiction. The goal is to make the addict see how his or her addiction is affecting everybody's life.

At first I thought it might be a surprise party, with all the people sitting in our living room, waiting for me to walk through the door. But the occasion was not my birthday. Everybody wanted to talk about my drug use.

My dad called it an intervention. He said all these people—he and my mother, my sister, my best friend, Angela, and even my history teacher, Mr. Harris—were there to help. It felt more like they were ganging up on me, and I told them so. I could see Dad take a deep breath, trying to stay calm. He introduced me to this guy, Ray, who was from a clinic in the next town. Ray asked me to sit down and listen.

They took turns. Mom said she was worried about my health, and Mr. Harris pointed out that because I'd skipped so many classes and failed to hand in assignments—in all my courses—I was in danger of flunking out. Angela and my sister talked about the time we almost got into a major car accident because I was driving drunk.

I couldn't believe they were bringing up all this stuff. Come on, it wasn't like I was proud of it. Nobody said I was a bad person, though, which I really appreciated.

Eventually, I started to believe that they might be kind of right. The only time I felt good was when I was taking the drugs, and even that didn't happen all the time anymore. I was tired of being so up and down and so broke. I hated it that my parents were always ticked off and that most of my old friends avoided me. I hated being so alone.

Mom had packed a bag with some clothes and stuff. She and Dad said that Ray could take me to the clinic right away. I figured that maybe it was time.

Those taking part in the intervention should have a close relationship with the addicted person. They can be family members, coworkers, or people with whom the addicted person spends a lot of time. Parents, friends, brothers, sisters, boyfriends or girlfriends, bosses, and favorite teachers are examples of people who could be in this group. Having someone, such as a counselor, act as a neutral party is a good idea too.

The point of an intervention is not to judge, but to try to get the addicted person to admit that he or she has a problem, and to seek help. You want him or her to face facts.

A successful intervention is one that is planned. Decide ahead of time who will say what, and in what order. Figure out some of the addicted person's arguments against what you're saying, and have reasonable answers ready.

Experts suggest staying calm, making sure the addicted person is not high and drunk at the time, and

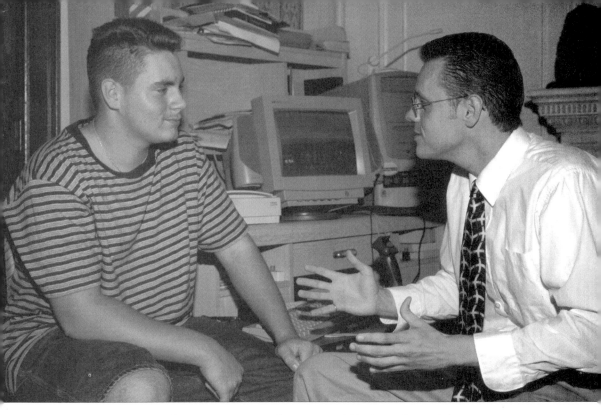

It is very difficult to recover from an addiction alone. There are many people an addict can turn to for help.

giving specific examples you know for sure are true concerning how the addiction has caused problems. Also, you should expect to face some anger and denial by the person who is the object of the intervention.

Types of Treatment

Once the addicted person admits there's a problem, it's time for treatment. While the person has to take part in overcoming the addiction, he or she cannot solve the problem alone. Treatment almost always means getting help from others.

The short-term goals of treatment are to reduce drug use and help the addicted person reenter society as a regular, involved member. Long-term goals revolve around lasting abstinence—ways to keep him or her away from drugs permanently.

Detox

Traditional treatment programs take several forms. Detoxification—detox for short—involves getting off drugs quickly and cleanly. You may know this method by its nickname, cold turkey. Many times detox takes place on an outpatient basis. The addicted person may have an initial short stay in a detox center or hospital, then return for appointments on a regular basis so that medical professionals can monitor the detox. The whole thing can last for a few days or a few weeks.

Counseling

Once the addicted person is off drugs, therapy starts, both to ease the withdrawal symptoms and to make the lingering cravings easier to handle. Counseling of this type can be either individual or with a group. The therapist and the patient talk about why the person may have started taking drugs and how to cope with problems without chemical help.

Inpatient Treatment

Another method of treatment is on an inpatient basis. In this case, an addicted person lives in a therapeutic community with other addicted people, in a clinic or home. They share chores and responsibilities, and often attend group therapy sessions in an effort to change any anti-social or criminal behavior associated with the addiction.

Experimental Methods of Treatment

Finally, there are controversial and experimental forms of treatment. One controversial method is to treat drug addiction with other, milder, less-addictive chemicals. Many drugs are being discovered and experimented with, but it is not known whether they actually work.

Methadone

Methadone is one drug that has been proven to help fight addiction. It is a heroin substitute that is taken in doses regulated by medical professionals.

Some people object to the use of methadone because the method does not cure addiction, and because methadone itself is mildly addictive. These people say that for an addict to simply change addiction from one drug to another is no solution to the problem.

Acupuncture

Acupuncture is another experimental treatment. Acupuncture is the use of needles to relieve pressure on certain parts of a person's body. It can ease the symptoms of withdrawal, making methods like detox much easier. Since it cures only symptoms, not the addiction, acupuncture is considered just a small part of larger treatment methods. Studies are still being done to figure out how effective acupuncture really is.

Relapse

Getting treatment is no guarantee that someone has recovered from addiction. People often slip and start taking drugs or drinking again. This is known as a relapse.

The major cause of relapse is uncontrollable cravings. Just because the addicted person has stopped taking the drug doesn't mean that the intense desire for it disappears. That craving could stick around for a long time—maybe even a lifetime.

Many things can trigger a relapse. If a person took drugs or drank because he or she felt sad or upset, feeling that way any time after treatment can make him or her want drugs or alcohol again. Sometimes being around people who are getting high, or with whom you used to get high, can start cravings too. Even certain rituals can make you want drugs again. For example, people who quit smoking but who used to have a cigarette with their morning coffee often feel a desire to smoke with that first cup.

Support

Because relapses happen so often, a person needs someone or something to count on—some type of support—to get over an addiction. Simply having a good friend or family member to talk to is a good start. Usually, though, it's not enough.

Talking with someone who has been in the same situation is one of the best ways to overcome an addiction. That is why twelve-step programs are so popular with those recovering from addiction. In these programs, groups of people with similar problems get

Support groups allow teens who are addicted to drugs to share their experiences and help each other stay clean.

together to talk about their bad days and their successes, as well as offer one another ways to stay clean and sober.

AA

Alcoholics Anonymous, founded in 1935, is perhaps the best known twelve-step program. People addicted to alcohol meet once or more a week for regularly scheduled meetings, at which members—who don't have to give their full names—are encouraged to discuss their addiction and how they beat it. Because getting hooked again is always a possibility, AA members are encouraged to attend meetings for the rest of their lives. In addition to having the support of a group, members can find a sponsor as well, someone on whom they can call for one-on-one help when cravings get to be too much.

Because of the success of Alcoholics Anonymous, other support groups have been created based on the way AA runs their meetings. Narcotics Anonymous (NA) and Cocaine Anonymous (CA) are two such groups. There are also Al-Anon and Alateen, which help families of alcohol abusers deal with their loved one's addiction.

Prevention

Experts agree that the best way to avoid addiction is to avoid taking drugs or drinking in the first place. Realistically, though, just saying no is not easy. Luckily, there is also a type of support that takes place before an addiction can start.

Prevention programs offer kids a chance to get away from situations in which drug abuse can occur. Often these take the form of after-school and evening activities under adult supervision. The focus is on teaching social and communication skills, building self-esteem, and providing education about the risks associated with drug use.

Prevention programs can take place in school, at community centers, or at home. Studies have shown that prevention on all those fronts works best. Parents or other adults who oversee the programs are frequently trained in the best ways to get the anti-drug message across.

The best way to avoid drug addiction is to avoid drugs and alcohol. However, if you are abusing one of these substances, it is not to late to get help. Recovery can be a long and difficult process, but it is possible. And it's worth it.

Glossary

abstinence Not taking drugs, particularly after treatment.

binge Taking repeated doses of a drug in a short period of time.

cannabinoid A scientific name for marijuana.

chronic use Taking a drug repeatedly, for a long time.

craving An intense desire or need.

cutting When a drug dealer adds harmless or harmful ingredients to drugs, to boost the weight in order to make more money.

dependent Unable to function without something; in this case, drugs.

detox (detoxification) A treatment method where the addicted person stops drugs quickly and cleanly.

experimentation Trying something for the first time, or first few times; testing.

inhalant A substance that gives off chemical fumes, which people breathe in to get high.

intervention When a group of caring people tell an addicted person how his or her taking drugs has affected all their lives; the object is to get the addicted person into treatment.

methadone A man-made heroin substitute used as a treatment for narcotics addiction.

neurotransmitter A natural chemical in our brains that sends messages to determine how we feel and react.

physical addiction When the body can't function normally without drugs.

prevention A support method aimed at stopping drug addiction before it can start.

psychological addiction When a person believes very strongly that he or she needs. drugs; getting mentally used to drugs.

regulate To oversee or control the amount and type of drugs a person takes.

relapse When a person who has stopped using drugs starts using them again.

therapeutic communities Places where groups of people trying to get over an addiction live, where they share chores and go to group therapy sessions.

tolerance The body gets so used to drugs it doesn't react to taking them; needing larger amounts to get high.

withdrawal The physical/mental sickness a person who is addicted goes through when he or she stops taking drugs.

Where to Go for Help

General Information/Hotlines

American Council for Drug Education
164 West 74th Street
New York, NY 10023
(212) 758-8060
(800) 488-DRUG (3784)

National Clearinghouse for Alcohol and Drug Information
P.O. Box 2345
Rockville, MD 20847-2345
(301) 468-2600
(800) 729-6686

National Council on Alcoholism and Drug Dependence (NCADD)
12 West 21st Street, 7th Floor
New York, NY 10010
(800) 622-2255

National Families in Action
2296 Henderson Mill Road, Suite 300
Atlanta, GA 30345
(404) 934-6364

Twelve-Step Programs
Al-Anon/Alateen Family Group Headquarters, Inc.
1600 Corporate Landing Parkway
Virginia Beach, VA 23454-5617
(804) 563-1600
(800) 344-2666
http://www.solar.rtd.utk.edu/~a/-anon
http://www.al-anon.alateen.org

Alcoholics Anonymous
http://www.alcoholics-anonymous.org/intgrp/00states.html

Cocaine Anonymous World Service Office (CAWSO, Inc.)
P.O. Box 2000
Los Angeles, CA 90049-8000
(310) 559-5833
Referral line: (800) 347-8998
http://www.ca.org

Families Anonymous, Inc.
P.O. Box 3475
Culver City, CA 90231-3475
(310) 313-5800
(800) 736-9805

Nar-Anon Family Groups
P.O. Box 2562
Palos Verdes Peninsula, CA 90274
(310) 547-5800

Narcotics Anonymous (NA)
P.O. Box 9999
Van Nuys, CA 91409
(818) 773-9999
http://www.wsoinc.com

Treatment Referrals
Boys Town National Hotline
(800) 448-3000
http://www.ffbh.boystown.org/Hotline/crisis_hotline.htm

National Association of Alcohol and Drug Abuse Counselors
3717 Columbia Pike, Suite 300
Arlington, VA 22204
(800) 548-0497

Substance Abuse Mental Health Services Administration
Information and Treatment Referral Hotline
(800) 662-HELP (4357)
http://www.health.org/phone.htm#phone

Web Sites
12 Step Cyber Cafe
http://www.12steps.org/

Students Against Drugs & Alcohol Web Page
http://www.sada.org

For Further Reading

Berger, Gilda. *Addiction*. New York: Franklin Watts, 1992.

Claypool-Miner, Jane. *Alcohol and You*. New York: Franklin Watts, 1997.

Colvin, Rod. *Prescription Drug Abuse: The Hidden Epidemic*. Omaha, NE: Addicus Books, 1995.

Glass, George. *Drugs and Fitting In*. New York: Rosen Publishing Group, 1998.

Glass, George. *Narcotics: Dangerous Painkillers*. New York: Rosen Publishing Group, 1998.

Gutman, Bill. *Harmful to Your Health*. New York: Twenty-First Century Books, 1996.

Phillips, Lynn. *Life Issues: Drug Abuse*. New York: Marshall Cavendish, 1994.

Ryan, Elizabeth A. *Straight Talk About Drugs and Alcohol*. New York: Facts on File, 1995.

Seixas, Judith S. *Living with a Parent Who Takes Drugs.* New York: Greenwillow Books, 1989.

Shuker-Haines, Frances. *Everything You Need to Know About a Drug-Abusing Parent.* Rev. ed. New York: Rosen Publishing Group, 1996.

Smith-McLaughlin, Miriam, and Sandra Peyser-Hazouri. *Addiction: The High That Brings You Down.* Springfield, NJ: Enslow Publishers, Inc., 1997.

Trapani, Margi. *Inside a Support Group: Help for Teenage Children of Alcoholics.* New York: Rosen Publishing Group, 1997.

Index

About the Author
As a writer and Editor, Jeanne Nagel has covered news, features, and profiles. In addition to a career in journalism, she has worked as a tutor, both privately and within a scholastic setting. She is currently the copy editor of a weekly newspaper in Upstate New York, where she makes her home.

Photo Credits
Cover photo by Brian T. Silak; p. 10 by Les Mills; pp. 30 and 41 © Mark Reinstein/Uniphoto Picture Agency; all other photographs by Brian T. Silak.